Novels by Wendy Koenig

One to Lose
Under Twin Suns

Poetry

Lions in the Closet
These Burning Stones

Anthologies

Breathe I, II, III, IV, and V
Sunlit Night, Coffee, and Sweet Dreams

Coming in 2015

Sentient

Fear, Swallowed

Wendy L. Koenig

Cadillac Press

Cadillac Press
185 Drummond St. Rd
Drummond, NB E3Y 1V9
Canada

Copyright © 2014 Wendy L. Koenig
All rights reserved
Printed in the United States of America

This book, or parts thereof, may not be reproduced in any form without permission. The scanning, uploading, and distribution of this book via the Internet or via any other means without the permission of the publisher is illegal and punishable by law.

2 4 6 8 10 9 7 5 3 1

FIRST EDITION

CONTENTS

Wilderness	1
Learning to be Poets	2
Poême de Terre	3
Poser	4
Who's Up Next?	5
Refugee	6
Where the Books Make My Life	8
Glow	9
Fade to Nothing	10
Nomad	11
Lemon Trees	12
Papillion	13

Pixels	14
Superhuman	15
Negative Space	16
What Love has Done for Me	17
Cotton	18
Heal Point	19
Prodigal	20
Chicago	21
Dine on You	22
Be Not Denied	23
River Baby	24
How to Build a Perfect Pie Chart in Florida	26
Betrayer	28
A Boy isn't Just a Boy	29
Pomme de Terre	30
Breathe	32
Pray for Rain	34
She Sells Seashells	35
Rain is Coming	36
A Lesson in Economics	37
I Will Remember You	38
Patrol	39
Stone Lion	40
Pink Coat	41

Bus 13	42
Boiling Water	44
Workhorse	45
Chronic Fatigue Syndrome	46
Grain	47
Break Away	48
Green Light	50
Asphalt Freedom	52

Pomme de Terre and *Pray for Rain* previously printed in *Upcounty*, University of Maine, Presque Isle, 2013.

Poême de Terre, Poser, Pomme de Terre, and *Pray for Rain* previously printed in *Breathe IV*, Cadillac Press 2012.

Breathe and *Asphalt Freedom* previously printed in *Upcountry*, University of Maine, Presque Isle, 2012.

Papillion, Stone Lion, Bus 13, and *Green Light* previously printed in *Breathe II*, Cadillac Press 2010.

Prodigal, Chicago, Breathe and *Asphalt Freedom* previously printed in *Breathe I*, Cadillac Press 2009.

For Mom

Fear,
Swallowed

Wilderness

My hands are restless on your skin,
riotous as dogs that roam
the hills behind our home.
As a child, I'd raided
that untamed brush, searching
for hen's eggs and a blind calf named
Daisy. She became my steed.
I rode, pulling her tail
for reins, knight of La Mancha,
jewels and gold to be found. My hounds
gave chase until they didn't.
Tonight, my fingers seek
gems of another kind in the wild
thicket of your chest. I am a crazed
troubadour, searching creek banks
for treasures, turtles, and frogs. You
are the dog, laughing at
my heels.

Learning to be Poets

Knife on whetstone,
our gaze sharpens
on lines of prose.
Soldiers in white jungle
territory. Amazon games
in the rain, we
hunt the original. In our
sleep, we hum electric thoughts
we slice through daily. We
burn pithy lines,
pollution in snow. We
build a pyre, toast our
tired feet and recite our
anthems to those
who listen.

Poême de Terre

Born out of a fertile
imagination,
the seed is planted.
It is watered by sweat,
tears and a sprinkle
of blood.
Hope and inspiration
warm the soil and the seed
sprouts.

Critique groups
thin it, cutting
away adverbs and
prepositional endings.
The claw out of the earth
the weeds of comma neglect.

The tender shoot
is fertilized
with scene details:
sight, sound, taste
love, fear
touch and smell.

The poem grows.

Seasons later,
it is harvested,
served on a plate
with eyes
that cannot see.
The words are cut
and dissected
into lists and pieces
that were never
the whole
of its truth.

Poser

Your cowboy slouch
tickles my nose
into a snort.
What did you do to deserve
     those boots?

Have you roped a steer,
     nestled the lariat under his horns,
     pressed heated iron to his leather,
     circled him back to the herd?
That triple ostrich and turquoise hat band
has never baked under a white
August sky, never
felt the sift
of red Colorado desert.

Ever strap a bedroll behind a saddle,
pull your brim low
and ride,
just ride?

That's how you find God,
you know.
You just ride until He's there,
ridin' beside you.
Then you stop
     and break open your kit.

Commune for a few days.

That's where the slouch comes from:
being driven by cattle, God and storm.
And riding. Just riding.
It's something you have to earn.

Who's Up Next?

Four blue shirts lean on
the white steel rail, flinch as
the bull drops his rider. Four
white straw hats, different
as night and day, tell the story.

The first hat, a sensible fellow,
flat with a bare bend down
in the back, over the neck,
to keep the wind from stealing it.
It's a full feeling, prosperous,
serious.

The last is like that first,
mimicking, yet more of a curve
toward the front, suggesting a
trifold, a free-thinker who only
emulates out of flattery and worship.

The third figures itself
a dandy, a ladies'
man. It sports a
laced brim bent
heavily in front and
back. A snake-skin
band matches
the rodeo decals
dotted over its surface.

The second hat harnesses a
devil-may-care attitude in its
conventional attire, but a
flippant curl traces
the wild hair below.
For him, it's all about the ride.

Refugee

There's a hurt there,
cut up, whited out like
an earthquake.
It tears me apart.
My life is more than
half gone. It has flown south
with my stolen passport.

These days, I'm half
human, afraid of spiders
that climb my hair from
root to crown. I am cowed
by green clouds,
like trains
that carry cargoes
of sneaky whirlwinds.
The glacier in my
backyard smokes
from our neighbor's fire.
It reminds me that pollution
in snow burns. So do
spiders from the sky.

I'm half writer, too, unsettled
by the struggle of a novel. You
lose the words if you
make them wait too long, you
know. I want to live like a native,
under coconut trees
and tanned skin, unafraid
to call them my own.

I want to be
Siamese twins. The first
rooted in the trials of my
youth. They were innocent
days not merely frittered away. No,
I flung them into every-
thing, a whore
for experience. My second twin
would be literary genius. Lavish
with pithy words, time,
and rhyme, a prostitute
for words.

Where the Books Make My Life

I live where the books
tower in tippy spires
from the floor.
Where the books
lie corded, stacked
high and flat on shelves
covered in dust.
Where the books
stand like soldiers, straight
and true. Where the books
are hospitalized: sunbleached,
broken, torn, glued,
       mildewed and foxed
Cherished books with faded
gilt letters, feather
insignias and yellowed
pages. Where the books
are leather or bound
in cloth, covered in jackets
or brown wrapping paper.
Where the books
cascade from piles
on the table and kitchen
counter. Where the books
make my life.

Glow

Today, the sun is three feet
deep, warming right through me
making translucent those hopes
I dare not whisper

I wonder idly if a stranger can
see them
if a fly can taste the quiet words
I speak to my future

Do they taste like honey mead or
stringent apple cider vinegar? What
would he think, if I could vomit
words on a page
like he vomits everywhere he pauses

Would he beckon the wind
to rail and growl?
To carry my words away?

Let the wind try to
carve the sun away.
My voice will stand.
The bottle of sentences within
ferments .

Fade to Nothing

My feet travel this
road, this always
bending, always

rearranging street
searching for you.
Burning fish rise and

fly from the pavement.
Trees of gold melt,
blacken snowflakes.

A woman dances on her
long blonde tresses.
She heard you in the park.

Children dressed in pink
coats run past
on their heads;

their feet pump the air.
Then I see you,
throwing stink apples

into the city from
an upside down plane.
The ship drops

from brilliant blue clouds.
It bumps onto the boulevard.
Then you are here

Nomad

Ice cream
pillow
under my tree
produces strategic
organic hieroglyphs and
erotic wanderings
in your memories.
Hallucinogenic
kisses in mine

Cotton-mouthed French
lips, soft as wine in a
half-drunk bottle,

trail through the outback
of your tangled
forest,
hide away
inside Chess
nights and Chinese
art.

Lemon Trees
a haiku

My lips pucker with
sweet longing made fragrant by
white lemon blossoms

Papillion

Quand ton tendre
amour a durci dans cette
chrysalide
d'oú seulement tu
émergeras parfaitement?

your tender
regard …
into this
chrysalis
from which   only you
emerge
perfect?

Love,
when did
your tender *amour*
durci
into this *chrysalide*
from which *seulement tu*
émergeras

        parfaitement?

Pixels

I breathe you,
though you're not here.

My fingertips touch glass,
but I feel your face,
soft and warm,
creased.

Your beard rasps against my cheek,
and your lips press warm against mine.

I open my eyes to see only pixels and words.
How many nights have I sat here,
waiting for your next whisper
to fill my screen?

Superhuman

The steam from last night
Fogged my brain
And I fell.
Like a pedestrian through a hole
In the street, I fell.
Like a clown at the top
Of the stairs,
I fell.
Like Newton's apple
      I fell.

I wanted to drown in your
Smile, make love to your
Natural musk. I wanted to
Climb
To the top of your
Office building, like
That mighty ape,
And shout to the world
That I fell.

I didn't.

But when you
Weren't listening, deep
Asleep, I leaned close
Whispered, "I love you."

Negative Space

He leans in, and
you try to shrug
away, always uncomfortable
in front of the lens.
No one sees the shooting pain.
Still, he holds you in place,
his giant paw draped over your
shoulder, and your smile develops in
resignation.

But it is the negative
space between your
body and his that tells
the story.

He's happy: family is everything, and
through him, your feel it, too.
But deep inside, you have always wanted
something more.

What Love has Done for Me

I married. I divorced. I
married. I divorced. In between,
I wrote poetry, answered
phones, guarded rich
bitch's homes. I loved. I
sobbed at the loss of another and
I grew to know my father.

Before it all began, I wrote
poems about apathy, injustice.
I caused two boys to fight. I rode
like a dust storm, drove
like a bank robber, danced
like a wind chime.

I found Jesus. Lost my
virginity. Found alcohol. Lost
my way.

I met a man who lit
my life from the inside.
We'll follow each other across
this globe. We share dreams,
passions and poetry.

Yet, there are some
things I cannot say.
Dark things rooted deep
in the hollows, deep
in the graves of my past.
These things are like
contagion and will burn
me to the ground.
Love keeps me mute.

Cotton

Navy blue words
fill my page,
scented in those
black mysteries I
try to escape,
but revisit
in the violence of my dreams.

My secrets are guarded
by a fire hot poker.
It lances those who
betray with false voice,
those who are invisible,
those who hide
in the iron
double-blind
storm above.

I am a white domino
swirling in a pale
gingham sky,
confused by
identical poets
with identical
nightmares.

Heal Point

Burgundy pear women
point true paths
through feral graves and
applications for dehydration.

Boot sunk souls,
they whisper to Thunder
Spirit mango, warming
huts, semi-flat
fungus, and
Churchill amber

Prodigal
*a dedication to Dylan Thomas using lines from his poem,
"Do Not Go Gentle into That Good Night"

Should burn and rage
fade away
with the dying of night

fork (no) lightning
cry (how) bright

Should wild men
cringe from
the sun in fright

grave men
near death

You can still
bless
blaze fierce tears
in the blinding light

Chicago

Black Cadillac
four badges
seven men dressed
for death

Thompson bullets spewed
into bricks
chuffed holes that cursed
men for generations

It was death valley
against that wall
Not murder
just Italian Business

Prohibition and a howling dog
named Highball
in Lincoln Park
St. Valentines Day 1929

Dine on You

I would fill my belly
with your tongue, lies and
improbable dreams.
I would roll your eyes
in my mouth, make
them see the pain you put me through.

Your yellow liver
would fuel my blood
in a rapture
of organic frenzy.
Your heart would be saved
for last, dipped in chocolate,
wrapped
in gold foil,
fricasseed with your
ever-wandering toes.

Be Not Denied

death waits
like a hollow
a pause
a playground in the dark

it itches to be awakened
before dawn

River Baby

Child
lost lamb
orphan seeking
love
and protection.
You
should have pro-
tected, guided
her from all
harm, not shove
her
into that loathsome
stinking
ice-encrusted
river
where only Leviathan
lives and
bears
witness.
He raises his
gnarled finger.
He will watch
for you and
every direction you turn
he will step into
your path and
bring you low.
He will destroy
your dreams
haunt your nights.
You, who
should have
guarded her

from boys
who court
long-legged
long-haired
blond beauties.

How to Build a Perfect Pie Chart in Florida

1. Ensure the prison and education budget
   come from the same wallet. Underpay
   teachers. Overfill
   classrooms.

2. Take 1143 convicts at the average age of 30.2: drug
   dealers, murderers, rapers of men, women and
   children. Those on Death Row. Ensure over half
   are WASPS,
   Jews,
   Irish or
   of Norwegian descent.
   A full one-third should be black.

3. Drop them into an empty zoo
   fit with bars
   and cages
   6 X 9 X 9.5.
   In hurricane season
   give them all passes to Disneyland.

4. Teach sex, dependency, caffeine, chronic illness, work,
   how to roll dice, lift weights, hide drugs, talk
   without stopping, how to chronically overeat, cut
   a man, crave a beating.

5. Take random drug tests and psychosocial addiction
   assessments.
   Enroll all the inmates in Substance Abuse programs.

6. Charge the inmates for every
   meal, every
   night, every
   privilege.

7. When his time is done, free the inmate, with contract to pay debt, into phobic society.

8. Repeat.

Betrayer

Cold-blooded lines of muscle
living corduroy,

rivers of firm flesh,
shift under our trespass.

Smooth coiled ropes
jerk into open-

mouthed pink cotton
candy surprise.

The king lifts his tail,
a scepter. His dusty hollow rattle

speaks to us like
a toy lures innocents.

A Boy isn't Just a Boy

Some farmer found Keith in a spring field
turned by the plow.
Turns out, the bad guys parked just up the road
at Lori's diner, drinking coffee and eating lemon pie.

Nobody really knows
what made the killers stop
to tell their story

Just a trust fund kid, they said.
They'd waited in the woods by the school four days
for the right boy.
Not finicky, they said. Just particular.

Pomme de Terre

The air is soft
up here.
It cushions the blows
of our economy,
never more than
depression wages.
The world staggers
from market turmoil,
but we –
>we struggle
>solidly on
>planting one foot
>in front of the other,
>like we plant our potatoes
>in long straight rows.

The rain falls gently,
slowing the rate
of our decomposition.
Our young leave
and never
return.
Or, if they *do*
it is only to raise
children
who abandon
our hope.
They follow our
water-driven
power,
exported
to another country.

The snow pours down
in fat flakes
driven deep as hell
by winds that remind us
we are alone.
Drifts as tall as our houses
muffle our cries of
injustice
indignation
as we are forced to live
by rules
that don't apply
set by distant people
with a different
lifestyle
who have never lived
on a harvester
sorting out rock and
rot,
reaching contentment
like a firm, round
potato,
earth apple,
from our own
Garden of Eden.

Breathe

My pencil scratches
        across this page
        these pores
        that beg to be filled
I smell
the pine forest
cut into
this fine wood
I see

        A woman
        long wheat hair
        sitting in the dark
        she searches heaven
        cries

superimposed
on this room

        There's a tiny body
        her daughter
        with the name of
my pencil scribbles:
                Alice

        There's a long flight
        basement stairs
        The woman sits
        beside the baby
        with the blue face

        With shaking fingers
        pushes
        on the white chest

blows a tiny
        puff
        of air
        into the baby's mouth

        again
        again

my hand shakes
the words dissolve into meaningless marks
        Still, she is there
        she looks to heaven
        once more
        leans in
        and whispers

I hear her:

        "alice"

        "alice"

        One last time
        she blows into
        her baby's mouth

        and the baby gasps

and I
can lay down my pencil

Pray for Rain

Bone white breasts,
your milk has dried.
Where will your children feed?
The corn has curled
like pineapple sticks;
      There will be no
        bread for supper.

Our pond is cracked earth.
The larders are empty.
Crops have been mown,
cattle sold.

The grass turns to dust.

We wait,
choke on our sweat
and watch the skies
in our land of cream and
honey.

She Sells Seashells
a broken sonnet

She digs for tiny cones, augers, olives and
whelks. She tastes the names in her mouth
and places them in the natty fishing creel
at her waist. It's the right way

to begin the morning, she says and smiles,
knowing you didn't start *your* day
in any similar semblance. She works
at money whenever she finds the time, and

would rather make open-faced cheese dream
sandwiches, explore the cove with frog-eyed
goggles, or paint the sunset as it coasts
on the ocean. She sways in a grass hammock

under the palms, writing novels
in her mind, pen and paper optional.

Rain is Coming

Wrists on the small of her back, trowel in hand,
my mother stretches the kinks loose.

An errant fly lands on her cheek and
her hand automatically brushes at it,
leaving a smear of mud like warpaint.

She bends to her young plants again, digging
new homes and curling tender roots into the dirt.

A Lesson in Economics

I grind broken
glass
into my heel
even as
your sharp
words
grind between my
jagged teeth

Ravaging
flames
sear my spine
fire my cheeks
My vision fills with wanton
density of smoke and I
search for one
pinprick of light
one magnificent
moment
that I can forgive

but none comes
and anger
blisters my walls
festering
until it explodes
in one consuming
orange blossom

Time travels on

and scorched earth
cools and sand
turns to glass
to spite my feet
again

There is no forgiveness

I Will Remember You

Yes to the dark uneven body of each
tree that dots this forest, this
home of individuals seeking community. Yes
to the deep channels hidden in weathered
bark. Vital secrets run in these rough
grooves, these valleys between. Yes
to roots that trundle underground
to seek dignity and calm. Yes
to weary branches that creak and scrape,
pushed by some cold wind. Yes
to pale leaves that shake with age,
clasp my hand and beg to understand.

Patrol

Time marches on
like an endless
column of soldiers

Some short,
breathtakingly —
    a moment
    of bliss —
erotic highs
not remembered years
later.

Tall soldiers
shorten their stride
trying to shorten
their time,
painful and choppy.

Fat soldiers
lumber, rolling
from foot
to foot:
a marriage
of highs and
lows.

Soldiers with snowy
crests understand
the meaning
of time
sharp enough
to know
it is only
the march
that matters.

Stone Lion

It was a killing
breath
deep in the belly
of that dragon.
After a century
of opening doors   of climbing
    that steep
        anyone hill,
I found myself somewhere
between sixty
and frozen.
Though not usually a fish issue,
I had too many days trying
to twist my mind
trying to crush the last load of
MY
American Night
beneath
a portrait
    of lies

Pink Coat

Wrapped in sugar cone
sweetness, do you know
what's rolling your way? That blonde
cocker spaniel at your side will be
your only friend. Tangle your baby
fingers in her glossy fur and hang on. Sunbleached
curls, golden wheat bent
by the summer rain - never trust anyone who
asks you to sing like Shirley
Temple or who loves unicorns,
fairies and elves. Pink wagon wheels
on your jacket show your future.
Little gypsy, you will want to know everything,
do everything,
go everywhere;
there will be no
patience for those in your way.
Wear only yellow rainboots and
let those cherry blossom wheels
roll you where they will.

Bus 13

It was you
who stormed
out that day
in a brilliant cloud
of anger and self-
righteousness you
who cursed the
driver kicked the
door swung down
the steps

And I watched you
hair flip from side-
to-side as you
strode to your house
your brush tagging
time with the beating
your daddy would give you
The driver's anger
followed you
to that tiny white
shack
because she could not
Twelve children whispered
held their breath
in seats as green
as a crocodile's back
when your daddy
stormed out his door
right past you
to the bus
fury bitten deep in his face

The woman driver
closed the door
and sped away
while you birded
the establishment and
your daddy roared
and the kids
cheered our shaking driver
at the corner

I looked back
at the two of you
your body stiff and rigid
preparing
your daddy barricaded but
hesitant

I understood your lie then
and knew you'd won

Boiling Water

The piercing whistle on the teapot announced its shrill readiness. My mother, masqueraded as the bumbling "Hortense McGillicuddy", climbed the long stairs to my attic bedroom. Gone were the ugly words, the blistering anger and the threats of disownment. Her charade coaxed my hot-headed fifteen-year-old rebellion to giddy laughter and playfulness. Arms looped together, we tromped down and down to the kitchen where she served the tea spiked with my forgotten handful of salt.

Workhorse

I shrink in a dark rectangled corner,
haunches on my heels. Spiders and centipedes
crawl through rotting gaps around the
printwork and bars to sun-warmed victory.
My seventy-pound head weighs heavy and I no longer
hear the critic's mocking cries while I wait for
recognition that does not come.

Chronic Fatigue Syndrome

Like a boxer's
punching
bag, my body
is weighted
deep.
When hit
too hard,
my seams
rip
open.
Sand
spews out,
forms desert
gales
that
drive
right
through me.
The air
scorches
my eyes. I
cannot see,
but through
a haze.
Grit
fills my
mouth, my
throat, my
lungs. I
cannot breathe.
It roughs me,
like sandpaper;
grooves form
into arroyos.
Still,
the sand
pours.

Grain

On the plain of me
there is nothing
but rain,
the refrain of distress,
and pain

the grain of my truth
is that you unwrap me
like a skein of yarn
warm comfort
      without strain
without stain – fresh
and
without chains

Break Away

Pylons sprout along the side
of the road
like the clusters of orange
striped tiger lilies
that surround your front porch

I'm missin' you

Late night
Joplin's wail strings out
my heart into a
thin wire
pushes my pedal
faster
past the snail
crawl of mammoth
logging trucks
and artillery transports

This monotone highway
pulls me
deeper into my goodbye
and Floyd shreds
What do you want from me?

There's no good place
behind me
and maybe no
good space in front

But I gotta go
gotta do somethin'
anything at all
before the undergrowth
of brush
roots me
in the peat-crusted cranberry bogs
of my forefathers
Joplin's voice shreds

Floyd's guitar wails
Thick-barked trees fence my road
stretch it

What do you want from me?

Green Light

My stomach clenches
giddy
with the thrill
My heartbeat thunders
in anticipation of action

Then it's me
and I jump
throw my arms wide
straight out to my sides
arch my back

No thoughts
as I dive toward the earth
Just the push of the wind
on my body
roar in my ears
I close my eyes and cry

I am the wind

Deep within my chest
I hear the call of the ancient Bald Eagle
She screams at me
at the world in defiance
                                          Fierce
Her claws extend before her
eye sharp and piercing
The blood of my ancestors boils with hers

I punch for the ripcord and my chute
catches air
jerks me upwards
The Earth falls away from my dangling feet

even as I open my eyes
I am a god
and servant
in silent worship of
the Earth below
and Heaven above

The Eagle within
drifts
high
in the currents of the breeze
She hungers for unfettered air
to feed
her freedom
I am at her mercy
cleaving to her breast

The blood of my ancestors boils with hers
And I scream at the world
in defiance

Asphalt Freedom

She was a pink Schwinn
tall and shapely like
that steed I'd named her after:
Fury

Long white banana seat
deep swoop to her frame
proud sissy bar
elegant flowered basket

I rode her
jockey on a desperate steed
with a blue jump rope
for reins

We'd charge from
far back in the alley
rubber hooves spinning
popping sharp gravel

Gallop down that AWESOME hill
to shoot wildly across the street
praying there were no cars
home to the awaiting spanking.

Wendy lives in New Brunswick, Canada. She was born in Colorado, but raised on a small homestead in Illinois. She attended University of Iowa, honing her craft in their famed summer workshops and writing programs.

Her first published piece was a short children's fiction, Jet's Stormy Adventure, serialized in The Illinois Horse Network. Since that time, she has authored and co-authored numerous books. Several of her novels and short stories have won international awards and have appeared in multiple venues.

Her poems have been printed in several publications, including *Upcountry*, University of Maine at Presque Isle's literary eZine, and several anthologies. This is her third book of poetry.

www.ingramcontent.com/pod-product-compliance
Lightning Source LLC
Chambersburg PA
CBHW060857050426
42453CB00008B/1002